WORLD ALMANAC® LIBRARY
OF THE
AMERICAN REVOLUTION

Soldiers and Sailors
in the American Revolution

Dale Anderson

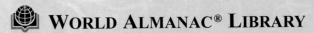
WORLD ALMANAC® LIBRARY

589000

Please visit our web site at: www.worldalmanaclibrary.com
For a free color catalog describing World Almanac® Library's list of high-quality books
and multimedia programs, call 1-800-848-2928 (USA) or 1-800-387-3178 (Canada).
World Almanac® Library's fax: (414) 332-3567.

Library of Congress Cataloging-in-Publication Data

Anderson, Dale, 1953-
    Soldiers and sailors in the American Revolution / by Dale Anderson.
      p. cm. — (World Almanac Library of the American Revolution)
    Includes bibliographical references and index.
    ISBN 0-8368-5929-4 (lib. bdg.)
    ISBN 0-8368-5938-3 (softcover)
    1. United States. Continental Army—Military life—Juvenile literature. 2. Great Britain. Army—Military life—History—18th
century—Juvenile literature. 3. United States. Navy—History—Revolution, 1775-1783—Juvenile literature. 4. Great Britain.
Royal Army—History—18th century—Juvenile literature. 5. Soldiers—United States—History—18th century—Juvenile literature.
6. Sailors—United States—History—18th century—Juvenile literature. 7. Soldiers—Great Britain—History—18th century—
Juvenile literature. 8. Sailors—Great Britain—History—18th century—Juvenile literature. 9. United States—History—Revolution,
1775-1783—Juvenile literature. I. Title. II. Series.
    E259.A53   2005
    973.3'092'2—dc22
                                                  2005040815

First published in 2006 by
World Almanac® Library
A Member of the WRC Media Family of Companies
330 West Olive Street, Suite 100
Milwaukee, WI 53212 USA

Produced by Discovery Books
Editor: Sabrina Crewe
Designer and page production: Sabine Beaupré
Photo researcher: Sabrina Crewe
Maps and diagrams: Stefan Chabluk
Consultant: Andrew Frank, Assistant Professor of History, Florida Atlantic University
World Almanac® Library editorial direction: Mark J. Sachner
World Almanac® Library editor: Alan Wachtel
World Almanac® Library art direction: Tammy West
World Almanac® Library production: Jessica Morris

Photo credits: Brown University Library: p. 9; CORBIS: pp. 7, 8, 20, 24, 27; The Granger Collection: pp. 11, 12, 15, 16,
17, 18, 19, 23, 30, 33, 35, 37, 39, 43; Independence National Historical Park: title page, p. 29; Library of Congress: p. 13;
North Wind Picture Archives: cover, pp. 5, 25, 26, 34, 40.

Printed in Canada

1 2 3 4 5 6 7 8 9 09 08 07 06 05

*Front cover: George Washington (center, on horseback), commander of the American Continental Army during the
American Revolution, leads his troops to winter camp at Valley Forge, Pennsylvania, in December 1777.*

*Title page: James Peale painted this portrait of George Washington on horseback in about 1790. He based the
portrait on a work by his brother, Charles Willson Peale—the faces of both the brothers can be seen on the left,
behind Washington. In the background on the right are Revolutionary soldiers, one carrying a French flag.*

Contents

In 1776, the thirteen British **colonies** along the eastern coast of North America declared themselves independent of Britain. The colonists were already fighting British soldiers in protest at British policies. In 1781, the British surrendered to American forces, and, in 1783, they formally recognized the colonies' independence.

A New Nation

The movement from colonies to independence, known as the American Revolution, gave birth to a new nation—the United States of America. Eventually, the nation stretched to the Pacific Ocean and grew to comprise fifty states. Over time, it was transformed from a nation of farmers into an industrial and technological giant, the world's richest and most powerful country.

An Inspiration to Others

The American Revolution was based on a revolution of ideas. The people who led the American Revolution believed that the purpose of government was to serve the people, not the reverse. They rejected rule by monarchs and created in its place a republic. The founders of the republic later wrote a constitution that set up this form of government and guaranteed people's basic rights, including the right to speak their minds and the freedom to worship as they wished.

The ideals on which the United States of America was founded have inspired people all around the world ever since. Within a few years of the American Revolution, the people of France had risen up against their monarchy. Over time, the people of colonies in Central

A VIEW OF THE TOWN OF BOSTON WITH SEVERAL SHIPS OF WAR IN THE HARBOUR.

The Americans who fought for independence faced the most powerful navy in the world. This woodcut shows British warships in Boston Harbor in 1774. They had been sent there in response to rebellious actions by colonists.

and South America, in Asia, and in Africa followed the U.S. example and rebelled against their position as colonists. Many former colonies have become independent nations.

The Americans

To win their independence in the American Revolution, the **Patriots** needed to form and train an army and a navy. This formidable task would take time and money, which the Patriots lacked. The Patriots faced other problems. American colonists were independent and not used to taking orders, making them ill-suited to serve as soldiers. In addition, the Patriots had a shortage of leaders with military experience. In the later years of the Revolution, the Patriots were supported by French troops, ships, and supplies.

The British

The British had one of the finest armies in Europe, but they had problems, too. Their supplies, equipment, and reinforcements were far across the Atlantic Ocean, many weeks away by ship. Morale was not always high among British troops. Some Americans—called **Loyalists**—fought alongside the British, but relations between the British and the Loyalists were not always smooth. The British (and, to a lesser extent, the Patriots) were also supported by Native Americans and African Americans.

CHAPTER ONE

Patriot Forces

Exactly how many Americans served on the Patriot side during the American Revolution is difficult to say. Many men enlisted more than once and are counted in records each time they signed up. A total of about 250,000 people might be a good guess.

The Size of the Army

American forces were weaker than that number might suggest. First, the total is spread out over many years of war. Second, at least half of those 250,000 men were in **militia** units. The units would be called up by their state to support the main army on a temporary basis. George Washington, who commanded the American forces, was desperately short of soldiers through-out the revolution as men came and went.

Forming the Continental Army

During the Revolution, the rebellious colonies (which became the United States in 1776) were

Departing Militia

"We are now left with a good deal less than half-raised regiments and about 5,000 militia, who only stand engaged to the middle of this month, when, according to custom, they will depart, [even though] the necessity of their stay be ever so urgent."

Patriot leader George Washington, January 4, 1776

led by the Continental Congress, a group of Patriot leaders drawn from all thirteen colonies. In June 1775, the Congress decided to form a combined army. The force was named the American Continental Army, and George Washington was placed in command. At that time, several thousand New England militia troops were around Boston, keeping the British trapped in the city. The Congress used those militiamen as the core of the Continental army and agreed to pay them. It also proposed recruiting **regular** soldiers to join the militias, who would not be able to serve long.

Militiamen made up a large part of the American military forces during the Revolution. This artist's impression shows soldiers from various units.

Recruiters were able to gather about 80,000 Continentals (members of the Continental army) and militia in 1776. It turned out to be the high point in troop numbers for the entire war. In the next two years, troop strength dropped by about 20,000 men per year. In 1778, however, the regulars were at their strongest, about 35,000 soldiers. Starting in 1777, they had agreed to serve for three years or the duration of the war.

Militia Units

Militia units fought from the war's first battles in the spring of 1775 to its end. Militias were formed by towns, counties, or the colonies that later became states. The fighters were part-time soldiers who spent most of their lives working on farms, in businesses, or in trades. They trained together, usually only a few times a year. In

Mixed Blessing

Militia units generally served with the Continental army only for a short period, agreed to in advance. Some only served in their own states, supporting the main army when there was a threat from the British.

The performance of militia soldiers was mixed. In several battles, such as those on Long Island in 1776, Brandywine and Germantown in 1777, and Camden in 1780, they simply threw down their arms and ran. In the war's first battle at Concord and Lexington, however, they carried out repeated successful attacks against the retreating British. They also helped win battles at Bennington, Saratoga, King's Mountain, and Yorktown.

periods of trouble, however, they trained as often as once a week.

Militiamen elected their own officers and sergeants. The soldiers, however, did not always take orders well. Indeed, the men often insisted on taking part in decisions.

This flag is the oldest complete flag known to exist in the United States. It may have been used by the militia in Bedford, Massachusetts, from the early 1700s and is believed to have been carried by them at the Battle of Lexington and Concord in 1775. The Latin motto *Vince Aut Morire* means "Conquer or Die."

Recruiting Men

During the Revolution, most forces included both Continentals and militia. Within the Continental army, there was a wide variety of conditions of service. Some soldiers were **drafted** by their state government. Others enlisted because they wanted to fight for the cause.

Many men who served long periods of time in the war were poor and owned no property. Some were hired

This watercolor of various American soldiers was painted by an eyewitness at the Battle of Yorktown in 1781. It shows (far left) a black soldier from the First Rhode Island Regiment.

African American Soldiers

Most African Americans who fought in the war took the British side, but hundreds also fought for the Patriots. Some were free blacks who believed strongly in the cause of liberty. Others were slaves who were promised their freedom for taking part in the war. Some slaves were placed in the army as substitutes for their owners, who did not wish to serve themselves. In 1778, there were nearly a thousand black men spread across every **regiment** of the Continental army. Black regiments with white officers existed in both Rhode Island and Massachusetts.

as substitutes to take the place of men who bought their way out of the draft. Others agreed to enlist because they were promised a **bounty**, for instance $10 and 100 acres (40 hectares) of free land. Some men signed up, collected the bounty, and deserted, only to enlist someplace else to collect a second bounty.

Separate Commands

Continental soldiers did not form one large fighting unit but were split into smaller commands. Small units manned forts or fought on the **frontiers**. Separate armies carried out operations in different areas. During 1780 and 1781, for instance, Washington had several thousand troops near New York City, while a few thousand more soldiers were in the South.

Training the Army

At first, the Continentals showed some of the same independence of spirit as militiamen. They were not used to military discipline or to taking orders. In the winter of 1777–1778, Baron Friedrich von Steuben arrived from Europe and began training the army camped at Valley Forge, Pennsylvania. Over time, the Continentals became a disciplined and determined fighting force. They showed this at the Battle of Monmouth in June 1778, after

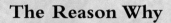

The Reason Why

"You say to [a European] soldier, 'Do this,' and he does it. But [to an American] I am obliged to say, 'This is the reason why you ought to do that,' and then he does it."

Patriot general Friedrich von Steuben, 1778

their long winter in camp. Although the battle ended in a stalemate, the Continental army fought effectively and showed the British that it was a force to be reckoned with.

The troops also developed a feeling of comradeship based on their shared sacrifices—the almost constant lack of food, supplies, and regular pay—and a belief that they were carrying the hopes of the country.

Different Types of Soldiers

The Continental army had a very limited **cavalry**, but it had three types of **infantry** units. The first type—the vast majority of units—was made up of ordinary foot soldiers.

The second type of unit was light infantry. These soldiers carried less heavy equipment and were meant to work as **skirmishers**, who went ahead of advancing armies and engaged in small conflicts, or skirmishes. Washington drew up rules requiring every regiment to have one company of light infantry that was fully manned and equipped. He hoped to assemble all the companies into one unit, but the plan failed to materialize.

The third type of infantry unit was made up of dragoons. These men rode into battle on horses, like the cavalry, but fought on foot.

Deborah Sampson (1760–1827)

Deborah Sampson was born in Plympton, Massachusetts, the oldest of six children in a poor family. Between the ages of eight and ten, she was sent off to be a servant on a farm, where she worked for ten years. Somehow, between household chores and farm work, Sampson managed to go to school. At the age of nineteen, she became a schoolteacher.

In 1782, Sampson disguised herself as a man and joined the Fourth Massachusetts Regiment of the Continental army, calling herself Robert Shurtleff. By the time she enlisted, most of the major battles of the American Revolution had been fought, and the war was coming to an end.

Sampson fought in a few minor battles, however, and received two wounds, one a saber cut to the head and the other from a bullet in the thigh. Knowing her identity would be discovered if treated for the gunshot wound, she refused medical care. Sampson's true gender was finally discovered when she became sick with a fever, and she was honorably discharged from the army in 1783.

Sampson returned home, married a farmer, and had three children. Her thigh wound bothered her for the rest of her life. Sampson resumed teaching and gave public lectures about her military service. She was later awarded a monthly pension for her service as a soldier.

An artist's impression shows American troops at the Valley Forge winter camp in 1778–1778, where they suffered bitter cold and hunger.

Perishing Army

"A country overflowing with plenty [is] now suffering an army employed for the defense of everything that is dear and valuable to perish for lack of food."

Patriot general Nathanael Greene, winter of 1779–1780

Camp Life

American army camps during the American Revolution were filthy, messy, unhealthy places. Regulars in the Continental army might have learned discipline on the battlefield, but they showed little in camp. They did not always use the **latrines**, and human waste could be seen in many places around the camp. They also dumped food scraps—when they were lucky enough to have scraps—anywhere they chose.

Washington constantly issued orders requiring his men regularly to change the straw they used for bedding, to eat healthy meals, and to bathe. The men were cautioned not to bathe for too long, however, because people at the time believed long baths might weaken their bodies.

Suffering in Winter

During the Revolution, most fighting stopped in winter and the men stayed in camps. Winters caused the worst suffering for the troops, especially the winters of 1777–1778 at Valley Forge camp and 1779–1780 at Morristown camp in New Jersey. Valley Forge has become legendary for the suffering of the soldiers, who were without adequate food, clothing, shoes, and blankets. The winter at Morristown, however, was actually worse, since the cold was more brutal and the lack of food even greater.

Pay Problems

Along with the lack of food and supplies, the Continental soldiers suffered other problems. They were paid very little—in fact, some militia troops received from local governments nearly six times what a regular soldier received from the Congress. Quite often, the Continental soldiers did not receive their pay at all because the government had no money. When they were paid, soldiers received Continental dollars, the paper money printed by the Congress to raise money for the war effort. But the value of that money plummeted throughout the war, and the bills that soldiers held became worthless.

Allies from France

After forming an alliance with the United States, France sent a few thousand soldiers to North America to join the fight. The first group of French troops arrived in 1779. The main body, numbering about 5,500, came in 1780. This force joined George Washington's forces marching to Virginia in late 1781. They helped win the Battle of Yorktown, the war's last major battle.

The French had regiments of infantry, two separate **artillery** regiments, and one unit that mixed soldiers of different types. This latter unit was called Lauzun's Legion and included infantry, cavalry, and artillery soldiers. The unit numbered about 600 to 900 men in all.

A print from the 1700s shows French troops disembark from ships at Newport, Rhode Island, to join the revolutionary effort.

CHAPTER TWO

British Forces

When the American Revolution began, the British government had to find extra soldiers for its army to send to America. Some of those additional forces came from recruiting, but the British also resorted to hiring foreign troops.

Regiments

The British army was organized into regiments. Each regiment had ten companies of about three officers and about sixty-five soldiers. The total size of a regiment was over eight hundred, counting all officers, soldiers, and support personnel. The support personnel included drummers, supply officers, and a surgeon.

Later in the war, the size of companies was increased, and two more were added to each regiment. Regiments rarely maintained their official size for long, however, as battle losses and illness reduced their strength.

The British liked to develop a strong spirit in each regiment. Each had its own name and number, such as the Eighth Foot Regiment. Some, like the Royal Welsh Fusiliers, had special names and long, colorful histories. Officers encouraged regimental pride, and the men displayed it in their behavior and uniforms.

Grenadiers and Light Infantry

Two of the companies in each regiment comprised **elite** soldiers. Grenadier companies had originally been formed in the early 1700s to hurl heavy, handheld bombs called grenades. By the 1770s, grenadiers had evolved into attack forces

Grenadiers were selected from the biggest, tallest, and strongest soldiers. This print from the 1800s shows a British grenadier from about the time of the American Revolution.

that used their size and power to overwhelm the enemy. Other nations had grenadiers in their armies, but British grenadiers were especially renowned.

The other elite company was the light infantry, the regiment's fastest and most agile soldiers. Their job was to move quickly and to cover the flanks, or sides, of the regiment when advancing. Sometimes these elite companies would be pulled out of their regiments and assembled to make a larger force of just grenadiers or just light infantry.

Poverty and Harsh Conditions

The ordinary soldiers in the army came from the lowest levels of British society. They were the poor, the landless, and the jobless. Many were former criminals who gained a pardon by enlisting. Some had been tricked into joining by recruitment officers who got them drunk. However they came to be in the army, British soldiers stayed in it for the rest of their lives. There were no retirements for foot soldiers.

15

Soldiers' Families

Even in America, the wives of married British soldiers lived with them in camp, as did their children. When the sons of soldiers reached fourteen, they were given the option of enlisting as drummers until they grew old enough to become soldiers. If they did not agree to enlist, they were kicked out of camp. The same happened to soldiers' daughters if they did not marry. When a soldier was killed, his widow had a month to remarry or she, too, was forced to leave the camp. Widows had to pay for their own trips if they returned to Britain.

*During the American Revolution, women and children who traveled with armies were called "camp followers." This group is traveling with a unit of German **mercenaries**.*

Pay was only a few pennies a day, and from that sum the paymaster withheld money to cover their food, clothing, laundry, and other expenses, leaving little for the soldier.

Punishments for breaking rules were severe. Soldiers might be confined in a windowless cell, beaten with sticks, or whipped for the most serious offenses. When the sentence was a large number of lashes, it was spread out over several days, with a maximum of 250 lashes being applied to the poor soldier's back each day.

British Officers

Officers came largely from the upper class. They were often the younger sons of nobles who had the money to buy a **commission**. A regimental colonel paid the king for the right to raise a regiment. He, in turn, sold the officerships. The price of a commission varied by rank—captains paid more than lieutenants—and according to the prestige of the regiment. Skilled officers could be promoted; incompetent ones could also advance simply by buying a commission for a higher rank.

Loyalist Troops

The British side also had units made up of Loyalists. The exact number who fought for the British is not known, but estimates range as high as 50,000 men. (This figure excludes

Banastre Tarleton was commander of a Loyalist unit called the British Legion. Tarleton—or "Bloody Ban"—was hated and feared by Patriots.

Steadiness and Spirit

"An action ensued in which our [Loyalist] militia behaved with a degree of steadiness and spirit that would not have disgraced any regular troops."

South Carolina Loyalist Robert Gray in an essay, "Observations on the War in Carolina," about the battle at King's Mountain, North Carolina, 1780

British general John Burgoyne addresses Native American troops before a successful attack on Fort Ticonderoga in July 1777. He demanded that they fight in a "civilized" manner, meaning that he wanted them to fight in the disciplined formations used by British soldiers.

African Americans and Native Americans, many of whom also fought on the British side.) Some joined the British army, while others formed Loyalist militia units. The British Legion was a force of Loyalists commanded by British officer Banastre Tarleton. It gained fame in the South for its fierce attacks on militiamen and on **civilians**.

Loyalist soldiers and officers received less pay than British soldiers. Even British officers did not receive full retirement benefits if they were in command of Loyalist troops.

Native American Troops

While some Native Americans fought for the Patriots, most joined the British because they hoped that,

if the British won, they would stop American settlers from taking more Native land. Native Americans, therefore, tended to take part in battles on the frontier. They sometimes fought on their own and at other times were attached to British units. Small groups of Indians also served as scouts for the British army.

At times, large bodies of Native American fighters moved and fought alongside a regular British army. Such an arrangement was not always pleasing to British commanders. They had difficulty controlling the Native Americans, who did not fight in the disciplined, orderly way that British officers were used to.

The most well-known Native American leader was Joseph Brant, a

Mohawk. He led a force of about four hundred Native Americans in a successful ambush of Patriot soldiers at Oriskany, New York, in August 1777. His raids in western New York made him a feared figure. The British eventually made him a colonel. In some battles, he led not only Native Americans but also white Loyalists.

Recruiting Mercenaries

Very early in the war, the British decided to hire mercenaries, foreign soldiers whose services were paid for by the government. The mercenaries that the British brought to America came from Germany, where several princes had highly trained, well-regarded soldiers. The British paid the princes a sum per head for their soldiers, and the princes got additional money each year they kept soldiers in the field. The soldiers themselves did not receive the money the British paid, and when soldiers were killed, the princes received another payment to recruit a replacement.

The Hessians

Nearly 30,000 German soldiers came to America as mercenaries. Many of them came from the Hesse-Cassel

A German man is forcibly enlisted for service by an army officer before being sent to fight in America. Fewer than three in five German mercenaries returned home after the Revolution.

region, and because of this all the German soldiers were referred to as "Hessians." Nearly 8,000 died, and many were captured. A large number, perhaps as many as 5,000, deserted. Many deserters and prisoners of war settled in North America after the Revolution.

The German regiments were organized similarly to British forces. They had one company of grenadiers for each four companies of ordinary infantry. They also formed companies of special soldiers called *Jaegers*, or hunters. These soldiers carried rifles and were considered expert marksmen. Altogether, the Germans had a reputation as excellent fighters.

The Attack

The British army were highly disciplined in the 1700s. Attacking soldiers marched, with shoulders touching, in lines three deep toward the enemy. At

Men dressed as British soldiers line up in ranks to reenact an attack during the Battle of Brandywine. The original battle took place in Pennsylvania in 1777.

50 yards (46 meters)—the best range for the **muskets** they carried—they stopped and took position. The front line knelt on the ground. The second rank stood behind them and slightly to the right, placing their left feet inside the right feet of the first rank. The third row positioned themselves the same way in relation to the second. The troops then blasted away at the enemy, each soldier firing about three shots a minute.

When the enemy lines wavered or weakened, the attackers charged with **bayonets**. The bayonet charge was meant to unnerve the remaining defenders, who would break and run rather than be stabbed to death.

Varying Success

These battle tactics succeeded in the open fields of Europe. During the Revolution, they produced some British victories where the land was open and even. Such tactics were less useful, however, in hilly or wooded areas, one factor that led to the British defeat at Saratoga in 1777. There, the British were an easy target for Patriot riflemen hiding among the trees.

Bravery at Bunker Hill

At Bunker Hill, Colonel John Stark of the New Hampshire militia commanded one part of the Patriots' lines. He set his men in three lines that would each take a turn firing and then reload their weapons. Stark kept his men from firing until the British advanced to just 50 yards (46 meters) away, making the American fire that much more destructive of the approaching troops. Finally, Stark ordered his men to shoot low so they would hit their targets.

The British advanced twice in the face of withering fire. The advances left nearly half the British troops dead or wounded, but they had the bravery to mount a third attack.

The courage of the British at Bunker Hill is even more remarkable in light of the fact that the Americans made a point of aiming for officers, who suffered a high percentage of **casualties**. That those soldiers continued their attacks without their officers shows the power of their training, regimental pride, and inner strength.

CHAPTER THREE

Uniforms and Equipment

The opposing armies in the American Revolution differed greatly in their appearance. Patriot militias typically did not have uniforms but marched and fought in everyday clothes. Some Continental soldiers wore ordinary clothes, too, but others eventually wore a range of uniforms. The British troops, on the other hand, were smartly dressed in their bright red and white uniforms.

Patriot Weapons

Soldiers on both sides carried muskets, with many American soldiers supplying their own guns. Other Americans received guns captured from British **arsenals** or taken from the battlefield. The Continental army also received over 100,000 muskets from the United States' ally, France, during the American Revolution.

The variety of arms used by Patriot forces led to supply problems because soldiers carried guns with barrels of several different sizes. Supply officers needed to find lead bullets, and the molds to make them, in different sizes as well.

American soldiers were supposed to provide their own **cartridge** boxes to hold cartridges and gunpowder. Some also brought knives or axes and **canteens**. Very few American troops had bayonets.

A New York artillery company, part of the Continental army, prepares to attack in Trenton, New Jersey, in 1776. Soldiers, traveling on foot, had to carry weapons and other heavy equipment.

British Equipment

Standard issue for all British soldiers was the musket they called the "Brown Bess." The bayonet on the musket was 14 inches (36 centimeters) long. British soldiers also carried a long sword and a short sword, a cartridge box with sixty rounds of ammunition, a knapsack with food, one or two canteens, and camping gear. All that equipment added up to 60 pounds (27 kilograms) to be lugged around while marching.

Rifles

Some companies were equipped with rifled muskets, or rifles. Rifles have grooves cut inside the barrel that causes a spin on the bullet to make it travel farther and more accurately. The rifles had limitations, however. They could not be loaded and fired as rapidly as ordinary muskets, nor were they equipped with bayonets.

British officer Patrick Ferguson invented a breech-loading rifle, in which the cartridge was placed in the barrel through an opening at its base instead of down the **muzzle**. The weapon could be loaded and fired rapidly, even in wet weather. The British army did not trust this new invention, however, and only about two hundred were manufactured.

Soldiers and Sailors in the American Revolution

Artillery

The armies also had artillery. They carried field pieces, which were relatively small and mobile, that fired 3-pound to 24-pound (1-kg to 11-kg) shells. Most were on wheels, but some sat on legs. Because field artillery pieces bounced when fired, soldiers called them "grasshoppers."

Successful Sieges

The armies also had larger artillery that fired shells weighing from 16 to 32 pounds (7 to 15 kg). These heavy

Firing a Musket

Several actions were necessary to fire a muzzle-loading musket. Soldiers began by selecting a cartridge, which held some gunpowder and a bullet. They bit off the end of the cartridge opposite the bullet and put a small amount of powder on the flash pan near the trigger. The rest of the powder was poured down the barrel through the muzzle. Using a ramrod, soldiers then rammed the bullet and paper cartridge down the barrel. Next, they aimed at the enemy and pulled the trigger, moving forward a mechanism that held a piece of **flint**. The flint struck the flash pan, igniting the powder there and causing a spark to enter a small hole in the barrel. The spark then ignited the rest of the gunpowder, and the resulting explosion propelled the bullet forward.

A man loads a Brown Bess musket during a historical reenactment of a revolutionary battle.

The British mounted a siege on the city of Charleston in April 1780. Their artillery shelled the city for several weeks until the Americans surrendered.

pieces were used during **sieges** to blast away at enemy fortifications. A major tactic in sieges was to dig trenches as close as possible to enemy lines and place heavy artillery in them. A few hours' firing by these weapons could convince a besieged commander to surrender. The British army used this tactic to win the surrender of Charleston, South Carolina, in May of 1780. The Patriots employed it to win at Yorktown, Virginia, the next year.

Patriot Uniforms

Most militia soldiers, other than those from Virginia, wore regular clothing rather than uniforms. This made for a varied appearance.

The first rifle companies, which showed up in Massachusetts in 1775 after the Battle of Bunker Hill, were formed in Pennsylvania, Maryland, and Virginia. The riflemen wore long shirts made of linen or buckskin that were loose fitting and long lasting. George Washington was immediately impressed by the practicality of this clothing and urged the Congress to adopt it as the army's uniform. The Congress rejected this unusual idea.

Continental Clothing

The Continental army had no official uniform for several years. In addition, when Washington took control of the new army in 1775, he noticed that there was no way of distinguishing between officers and enlisted men. He ordered officers to wear plumes or badges of different colors to show their rank.

Uniforms became more widespread in the Continental army after 1778, when they were delivered in bulk from France. The breeches (or pants that end just below the knee) and waistcoats were white. Coats came in brown or blue. Not until 1779 did

Different units of the Continental army trimmed their uniforms in varying colors. Officers wore plumes in their hats. The buckskin outfit (fourth from right) was typical for independent companies of riflemen.

the Congress make blue the official color of the Continental uniform. The Continentals continued, however, to vary their uniform. The Delaware Continentals wore blue coats with red trim. Lee's Legion was a special unit that combined cavalry and infantry under the command of Henry Lee of Virginia. Formed in 1780, the Legion was dressed in distinctive green jackets.

British Soldiers

From bottom to top, meanwhile, the British soldiers' uniform was handsome but impractical and uncomfortable. Regimental officers could require many particular touches meant to make the uniforms more picturesque and stylish. Often these personal touches simply added to the soldiers' discomfort.

Above their socks and shoes, the soldiers wore breeches. Next came a waistcoat with buttons. The waistcoat and breeches were white or tan, and both had to be kept clean. Dirty clothing was punishable by flogging, even in the muddy surroundings of the battlefield.

Bright Red Coats

On top of the waistcoat, the British soldiers wore the bright red coats from which they got their nickname, "the Redcoats." These coats usually had long tails that almost reached the knees, although light infantry troops wore short jackets that were much more convenient in a fight. In addition, the coats were cut small, pinching the soldiers' arms, back, and chest. The discomfort was increased when

Demon Tailors

"The uniform of the British soldier in 1775 might have been designed by some demonic tailor who had sworn **sartorial** vengeance upon the human frame.'"

Historian David Hackett Fischer,
Paul Revere's Ride, *1994*

The Officers' Uniform

Officers' coats were scarlet, made with an expensive dye that kept its color longer than the cheaper dye used for lower ranks. Officers also wore metal medallions wore around their necks. These scarlet coats and shiny medallions made officers stand out from their men—and offered tempting targets to Patriot marksmen.

Other Uniforms

The uniforms of Loyalist regiments looked like those of the British Redcoats, but they were green with white trim. Most French soldiers wore coats that were a showy but impractical white. The Germans' uniforms were mostly blue, but *Jaeger* units wore green coats trimmed in red.

In a revolutionary battle reenactment, participants wear the uniforms of the British Redcoats.

the coats got wet and shrank. The fabric of the coat was tough and long lasting. Over the coats, soldiers wore two belts that went diagonally from shoulder to waist and formed a cross.

Hair and Headgear

Even a British soldier's hair was uncomfortable. The colonel who commanded each regiment could tell troops how to wear their hair. Some preferred their men to powder their hair to make it white. Others wanted men to shape their hair in some way, which required the soldiers to cover their heads with grease.

British soldiers had three kinds of headgear. All of them were uncomfortable. Grenadiers wore tall black caps made of bearskin that were also top-heavy. The light infantry had leather caps that shrank when wet. Regular troops wore a three-cornered hat that was worn small and had to be taped on to make it stay in place.

CHAPTER FOUR

Food and Supplies

Throughout the American Revolution, both sides had difficulties keeping their armies fed and supplied. The Americans lacked supplies and money. The British suffered their own problems, including the distances that supply ships had to travel.

Continental Army Supplies

When the war broke out, only two industries of any size existed in America—iron production and shipbuilding. The latter proved useful for creating a navy, although only a small one. Iron foundries were useful, too, but the Patriots lacked factories that could turn raw iron into finished products. A new gunpowder industry developed, but the powder was of poor quality.

The Patriots managed to capture some supplies from British ships and arsenals, but it was never enough. For vital supplies, therefore, the militia and Continental army relied on handmade products. The country had gunsmiths, but they did not produce enough guns to meet the armies' needs.

Bare Feet and Tatters

"Here comes a soldier, his bare feet are seen through his worn-out shoes, his legs nearly naked from the tattered remains of an only pair of stockings . . . his shirt hanging in strings."

Patriot doctor Albigence Waldo, diary entry,
Valley Forge winter camp, December 14, 1777

General Nathanael Greene held the difficult post of Continental army quartermaster general for over two years. He was in charge of all supplies except food and clothing, which was the responsibility of the commissary general.

Many dedicated women across all the states devoted themselves to sewing uniforms, but they were unable to make clothes for the whole army.

Supplies for the British

The British suffered problems early in the war when the navy refused to haul supplies for the army, forcing the army to compete with it for ships and sailors. Eventually, the British reorganized their supply efforts and made the system work more smoothly.

Feeding the Continentals

The Continental army's first commissary general—the officer in charge of food and clothing—was Joseph Trumbull. He succeeded at first in keeping the army fed. Once the Continental army moved south from Boston to New York in the spring of

How the Armies Survived

When food supplies were short, as they often were, armies on both sides survived by seizing grain and animals from farms near their camps. Sometimes they stole the food, and other times they paid for it. Washington issued strict orders, not always followed, that soldiers should pay for the food they took or, at the very least, leave a receipt so farmers could make a claim on the government. He felt that treating civilians fairly would help build loyalty to the Patriot cause. Farmers, however, wanted nothing to do with the money issued by the Continental Congress. They were happier when British soldiers arrived because, when the British paid, it was with gold or silver coins.

General Washington and his staff welcome a wagon train bringing supplies for the army.

Bearing Hardships

"This evening we had our general's applause for our fortitude to bear hardships with patience, especially the want of provision, meat being out, and our bread but poor."

Continental army doctor Josiah Atkins, diary entry on march to Virginia, June 15, 1781

1776, however, General Trumbull's supply system fell apart.

The Congress promised each soldier a pound (0.5 kg) of beef, pork, or salted fish, a pound (0.5 kg) of bread or flour, and a pint (0.5 liter) of milk every day. It also pledged to supply peas or beans, rice or cornmeal, and other foods every week. These standards were rarely if ever met. Often the soldiers received just flour, reducing them to eating "fire cakes"—flour mixed with water and shaped into a patty to be cooked over a fire. The poor quality of this diet made soldiers vulnerable to the diseases, such as smallpox and dysentry, that plagued the army throughout the war.

Hungry British Soldiers

The British army spent several winters in cities such as Boston, New York, and Philadelphia. All were ports that could be reached by British supply ships. The sheer quantity of shipped food, including flour, meat, and cheese, was impressive—about a third of a ton of food per soldier per year. Despite the large amount of food shipped, however, British soldiers sometimes went hungry, and they also suffered from sickness in large numbers. Fresh produce was hard to come by during those winters, and supply ships were sometimes delayed.

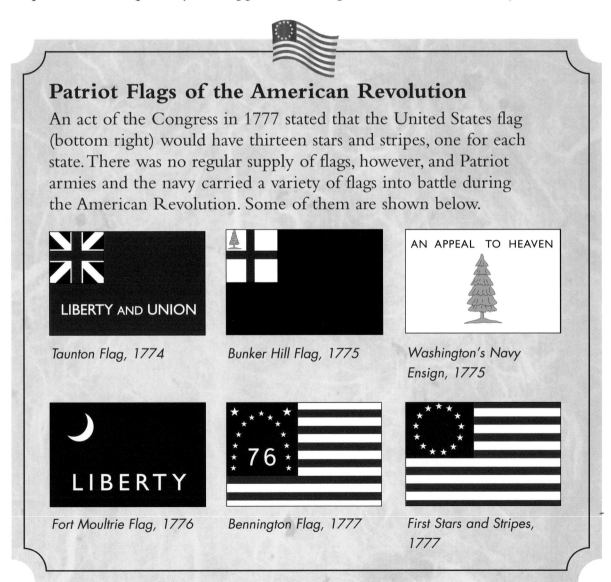

Patriot Flags of the American Revolution

An act of the Congress in 1777 stated that the United States flag (bottom right) would have thirteen stars and stripes, one for each state. There was no regular supply of flags, however, and Patriot armies and the navy carried a variety of flags into battle during the American Revolution. Some of them are shown below.

Taunton Flag, 1774

Bunker Hill Flag, 1775

Washington's Navy Ensign, 1775

Fort Moultrie Flag, 1776

Bennington Flag, 1777

First Stars and Stripes, 1777

CHAPTER FIVE

Supporting the Armies

Wars are won or lost by the performance of armies in the field, but the armies depend on the support of others. Supply officers must provide a steady flow of food, clothing, ammunition, and equipment. Other people—staff officers, doctors, and spies —contribute to the effort as well.

Army Staffs

Commanding officers had aides to help them in their work. In the British army, these officers were called adjutants. The adjutant made sure the general's orders were being followed. Generals also had aides who carried orders to the commanders of units within their armies and brought information back to the generals during battles.

Medical Care

Medical care in the 1700s was a haphazard business. Doctors did not have the training they have today, and they lacked good instruments and medicines. People did not yet understand that germs caused disease or that wounds could become infected. This lack of knowledge led to many deaths during the Revolution.

Both sides in the war placed a surgeon with each regiment. The care they gave soldiers was not very impressive. It was common for surgeons to

While he was leading the Continental army, Washington picked the twenty-year-old Alexander Hamilton, later the country's first secretary of the Treasury, to be his top aide. Hamilton, pictured here at the siege of Yorktown in 1781, served in the post of aide for more than four years. He and Washington developed a close relationship.

bleed patients who were ill or even wounded. Bleeding was the practice of deliberately cutting a patient to let blood flow. It was thought to remove diseased or weak blood from the body. Remarkably, some soldiers survived this treatment.

Wounds and disease were major causes of death. The Congress member (and future president) John Adams once lamented that disease killed ten times more soldiers than the enemy did. Smallpox, dysentery, measles, malaria, and scurvy were all killers. Some soldiers died from infections caused by dirty medical instruments.

Field Hospitals

"This hospital is now crowded with officers and soldiers from the field of battle. . . . The foreigners are under the care and management of their own surgeons. I have been present at some of their . . . operations, and remarked that the English surgeons perform with skill and dexterity."

Continental army doctor James Thacher, diary entry, October 24, 1777

A woman invites a British officer to tea in the hope of getting information to help the Patriot cause.

Seized Papers

"Original dispatches and papers which might be seized and sent to us. . . . Number and position of troops, whence and what reinforcements are expected and when—including persons of rank."

Major John André of the British army, outlining information wanted from Patriot traitor Benedict Arnold, May 10, 1779

Female Spies

Both sides had spies that infiltrated the ranks of the other side to get information. At the beginning of the Revolution, Patriot leaders in Boston knew that the British were planning to march to Concord, Massachusetts, to seize supplies because someone close to British commander General Thomas Gage told them. Historians believe that this spy was, in fact, Gage's American wife, Margaret.

Ann Bates of Philadelphia spied for the British by entering Patriot camps to sell needles, knives, and other goods.

An unknown woman, identified only as "Miss Jenny" in British records, spied on the French for the British. Another mysterious woman, known simply as "355," spied on the British in New York for the Patriots. She was arrested after Continental army officer Benedict Arnold switched sides and told the British she was a spy. She apparently died in prison.

The Culper Ring

The woman known as 355 was part of an elaborate spy network called the Culper Ring. Formed by Patriot Benjamin Tallmadge in 1778, it had

James Armistead Lafayette (c. 1760–1830)

Born into slavery, James Armistead became one of the Patriots' most important spies in the last major struggle of the war. Joining the army with the permission of his owner, Armistead was recruited by Continental army general the Marquis de Lafayette to spy on British general Charles Cornwallis at Yorktown, Virginia.

Armistead entered the British camp and offered to work as a laborer. Once there, he learned as much as he could about British plans. His work was made easier when Cornwallis recruited him to spy on the Patriots. Armistead pretended to do so while continuing to pass information to the Patriots. After the war, Armistead returned to slavery. At Lafayette's urging, the Virginia legislature granted him his freedom in 1786 or 1787. Armistead changed his name to Lafayette. Many years later, he received an army pension in recognition of services to his nation.

many members who reported on British movements and plans by spying on officers at their headquarters in New York. The spy ring included the operator of a coffee house and the manager of a clothing shop that British officers visited.

Other people also helped the armies, even though they were not officially spies. Farmers, city dwellers, and other civilians who had seen enemy troops in their area could pass word to the other side.

Camp Followers

In the British army, wives and children of soldiers were allowed to stay with their husbands in camp. They trailed behind an army on the march and were known, therefore, as "camp followers." The wives could earn small sums of money by cooking and doing laundry or other chores.

Patriot women sometimes accompanied their husbands in the army, too. This was less likely for farm wives, who tended to stay home to keep the farm running. But the Continental army was full of men who had no property, and their wives often went with them, doing similar work to that done by the wives of British soldiers.

Life was difficult for camp followers. Tents or shelters were crude, and there was little bedding. Food was scarce, and there was hardly any extra

Motley Crew

"Here was a motley crew, covered with rags and filth, visages pallid with disease, emaciated with hunger and anxiety, and retaining hardly a trace of their original appearance."

Patriot soldier Ebenezer Fox, describing a British prison ship

for women and children. As was the case with soldiers, many camp followers died from disease and lack of food.

Prisoners of War

The armies also needed people to guard the prisoners they captured and to run camps for prisoners of war. Throughout the war, neither side really had the facilities and resources to house, clothe, and feed the growing number of prisoners they took.

Conditions got particularly bad when there were large surrenders. About 4,000 Patriots became prisoners when the British captured New York City in 1776; another 5,000 were added with the surrender of Charleston, South Carolina, in 1780. Patriots captured 5,000 British and German soldiers at the Second Battle of Saratoga in 1778 and nearly 8,000 prisoners after the Battle of Yorktown in 1781. These huge numbers strained the crude prison systems.

Prison Camps

The British kept most of their prisoners in New York City, which they held until the end of the war. Prisoners were placed in warehouses, churches, and some of the buildings of King's College (now Columbia University). Thousands of Patriots were placed on prison ships in New York Harbor. Conditions on these ships were particularly miserable. Filth and lack of food led to widespread disease. The exact number of prisoners who died on the prison ships is unknown, but estimates say it was 8,000 to 11,000.

Patriot prisons were not much better, although with a constant manpower shortage, security was not tight. Many prisoners could simply walk out of the camps. Patriots had few objections when captured Germans did this because the mercenaries tended to hire themselves out as farm hands rather than returning to fight for the British. Patriots treated Loyalist prisoners more harshly. In the North, some Loyalists were held in a Connecticut mine. Others were shipped away from their home states and held in miserable conditions.

The British prison ship Jersey *was anchored off Brooklyn, New York, during the British occupation of New York City. Prisoners were kept in terrible conditions.*

CHAPTER SIX

The Navies

The American Revolution was chiefly a land war, but navies did play significant roles. The main navies were the British Royal Navy and the American Continental Navy, set up by the Congress in 1775.

The British Navy

The British had the strongest navy in Europe. British ships brought soldiers, equipment, and supplies across the ocean so they could fight. They also ferried messages back and forth between the government in London and generals in the field. The British navy moved troops to New York, Philadelphia, and the South to help carry out major new British offensives.

Losing Resources

During the Revolution, Patriots captured hundreds of British supply ships, gaining vital resources for their cause and denying those resources to British armies. The British navy

Naval Superiority

"No land force can act decisively unless it is accompanied by maritime superiority. . . . For proof of this, we have only to [look at the ease] with which the British shifted their ground, as advantages were to be obtained at either extremity of the continent, and to their heavy loss the moment they failed in naval superiority."

George Washington, letter to Patriot general the Marquis de Lafayette after the Battle of Yorktown, 1781

In September 1781, French sailors drove off a British fleet in the Battle of the Chesapeake Capes in Chesapeake Bay. The French action deprived British soldiers at Yorktown of a means of escape, and the British surrendered to the Americans in the Battle of Yorktown a few weeks later.

also lost access to American resources that they used to build ships. For decades, the navy had depended on pitch and tar taken from trees in North Carolina for waterproofing. Pines in New England had been perfect material for tall, straight masts. Britain was short of good hardwood for building and repairing ships, but the rebelling colonies had previously supplied them with abundant oak.

(Eventually, Britain filled these needs with lumber from Canada and the lands along the Baltic Sea.)

British Sailors

The British had another problem, too—filling their ships with sailors. Desertions were common, in part because sailors resented having been forced into the navy in the first place. To fill crews, the navy sent teams

Privateers

Although the Continental navy was small, it was able to sink or capture nearly 200 British ships. Even more damage was done by American privateers. These were privately owned ships ordered by the government to capture enemy merchant ships and take their cargoes (frequently consisting of supplies for the British army). The proceeds from the sale were divided among the privateers' owners, officers, and crew. While the Continental navy had only 60 or so ships, nearly 1,700 American privateers sailed. Privateering proved very profitable for the crews. They captured hundreds of ships, damaging British naval operations. But it was a dangerous business— the British threatened to treat privateers as pirates, which meant they could be hanged. No Americans were ever executed, but the crews of captured privateers were treated very harshly.

A recruiting office for privateers in New London, Connecticut.

called press gangs along city streets. These gangs would simply seize men and force them to join. They also took sailors from merchant ships and from jails. Another reason sailors deserted was their low wages, the same monthly amount that had been set in the 1600s. Worse, they were often not paid even this paltry sum.

Thousands of sailors were constantly on the lookout for a chance to escape from the British navy. The British took steps to try to prevent their deserting. Some ships, when reaching a port, would transfer their crews to another ship scheduled to go out to sea. That way, the sailors would never set foot on shore, where it would be easier to escape.

The Continental Navy

Most American seamen and captains came from the northern states, where the colonial shipping industry had been based before the war. When they were given a newly built ship, American officers were expected to recruit their own crews.

The Congress set out detailed rules for conduct aboard the ships. They provided for somewhat gentler treatment of sailors than that under British rules. One regulation said that no sailor could be given "any punishment beyond twelve lashes upon his bare back with a **cat-o'-nine tails**" unless he had been found guilty of

Navy Rules

"Whenever a captain shall enlist a seaman, he shall take care to enter on his books the time and terms of his entering, in order of his being justly paid."

"Rules for the Regulation of the Navy of the United Colonies," November 1775

an offense by a **court-martial**. (The Royal Navy had a similar rule, but captains routinely ignored it.) On the other hand, the Congress ordered captains to place a wooden collar around the neck of sailors caught cursing (a rule that was probably rarely enforced).

British Naval Uniforms

Ordinary British seamen of the period, unlike regular soldiers, had no set uniform. Most avoided the coats with long tails that were fashionable because the tails could be whipped by the wind and become entangled in the ship's rigging. Also useless were shoes, which made climbing the ship's rigging difficult. Sailors simply went barefoot. Similarly, the buckles or ties that fastened breeches below the knees proved awkward at sea. They were usually abandoned in favor of loose-fitting pants that ended just below the knees, which were called "slops." Sailors did wear coats and socks when

Out of Service

Periodically, a ship would have to be beached to clean its bottom of barnacles and seaweed. This complex process took a long time and took the ship out of service. During the war, the practice of covering ships' bottoms with copper became more widespread. Barnacles did not attach to ships built this way.

it got cold, and they often sported handkerchiefs around their necks.

Some captains wanted standard uniforms for the men who rowed the small boats that ferried them between ship and shore. Those captains had to pay for that clothing out of their own pockets. Naval officers did have uniforms that differed for each rank.

Ignoring the Congress

Officers and sailors in the Continental navy dressed similarly to British seamen. When the Congress created the navy in October 1776, it said officers' uniforms should be blue with red trim. The navy captains met in May of the following year, however, and

decided to adopt instead a blue and white uniform similar to that worn in the Royal Navy.

Ships' Quarters

The quarters on ships in both the American and British navies were small and cramped. Sailors slept in hammocks. Most officers had beds that were thin mattresses stuck into a hole in the wall. Captains, of course, had their own cabins.

Food was not very good and consisted largely of biscuits and salted meat that often contained maggots. Fresh fruit and vegetables could only be obtained at ports during harvest time. Captains and their officers had better fare than ordinary sailors.

Duties on Board

Officers and crew in both navies were split into six groups called watches. Each watch had the task of taking charge of the ship for four hours at a time. A sailor's daily routine included cleaning the decks and making sure that rigging and sails were in good shape. Guns would need to be cleaned, and occasionally the crew carried out gunnery practice.

Much of the work done on board naval ships was dangerous. When it came time to unfurl sails, sailors had to clamber up the rigging to each of the yards, which were the horizontal wooden pieces that held the sails.

There, while hanging onto the yard with one hand, they had to use the other to untie the ropes that kept the sail gathered. In rough seas, they could easily be pitched to the deck or into the water.

This picture shows Patriot naval hero John Paul Jones and his crew capturing the British warship Serapis *in September 1779. You can see sailors on the rigging in the background.*

Time Line

1775   April 19: Battle of Lexington and Concord.
June 14: Continental Congress creates American Continental Army.
June 15: Congress names George Washington as commander of Continental army.
June 17: Battle of Bunker Hill.
July 2: Washington takes command of Continental army.
October 25: Congress creates American Continental Navy.

1776   March 17: British evacuate Boston.
March 23: Congress authorizes privateers to attack British shipping.
July: First German troops reach North America.
July 4: Congress approves Declaration of Independence.
August 27: Battle of Long Island.
November 16: British capture Fort Washington.
December 26: Washington captures German post at Trenton, New Jersey.

1777   January 3: Washington defeats British at Princeton, New Jersey.
August: Battle of Oriskany.
August 16: Battle of Bennington.
September 11: Battle of Brandywine.

September 19: First Battle of Saratoga.
September 26: British capture Philadelphia.
October 4: Battle of Germantown.
October 17: British surrender at Saratoga.
December 17: Washington's army enters winter quarters at Valley Forge.

1778   February 6: United States and France sign treaty of alliance.
February 23: Friedrich von Steuben arrives at Valley Forge.
May 8: Henry Clinton named to command the British forces in the Americas.
June 18: The British begin to leave Philadelphia and march to New York City.

1780   May 12: Patriots surrender Charleston, South Carolina.
August 16: Battle of Camden.
October 7: Battle of King's Mountain.

1781   Battle of Cowpens.
September 5: Battle of the Chesapeake Capes.
October 19: British army surrenders after Battle of Yorktown.

Glossary

arsenal: store of weapons and ammunition.

artillery: large heavy guns, such as cannons.

bayonet: blade attached to front end of a shoulder gun and used to stab the enemy in combat.

bounty: money paid as a reward.

canteen: container for carrying drinking water or other liquids.

cartridge: case or shell that holds gunpowder and bullets for use in a firearm.

casualty: soldier or other person who is wounded, killed, or missing in battle.

cat-o'-nine-tails: whip with nine cords.

cavalry: soldiers who traveled and fought on horseback.

civilian: person who is not in the armed forces.

colony: settlement, area, or country owned or controlled by another nation.

commission: certificate that gives a person a position as an officer in an army or navy.

court-martial: trial of a member of a military force.

draft: order a person to join a military force.

elite: treated as special and superior.

flint: rock or other material that produces a spark when it strikes iron or steel.

frontier: edge of something known or settled. In the early years of the United States, the frontier meant the most westward point of white settlement.

infantry: soldiers who traveled and fought on foot.

latrine: pit dug for use as a toilet.

Loyalist: American who rejected independence and wanted the colonies to remain British.

mercenary: soldier who serves just for money, especially one hired by a foreign country to fight on its behalf.

militia: group of citizens organized into an army (as opposed to an army of professional soldiers, or regulars).

musket: type of shoulder gun usually carried by infantry during the Revolution.

muzzle: open end of a gun from which the shot comes out.

Patriot: American who supported the American Revolution; more generally, a person who is loyal to and proud of his or her country.

regiment: unit in an army made up of a varying number of companies. Several regiments make a brigade.

regular: professional soldier; member of a national army.

sartorial: having to do with clothing.

siege: military operation in which a group of attackers surrounds a target and either attacks it or keeps it trapped in an attempt to force it to surrender.

skirmisher: fighter who engages in a minor fight during a war or battle.

Further Resources

Books

Allen, Thomas B. *George Washington, Spymaster: How the Americans Outspied the British and Won the Revolutionary War.* National Geographic Children's, 2004.

Cox, Clinton. *Come All You Brave Soldiers: Blacks in the Revolutionary War.* Scholastic, 1999.

Martin, Joseph Plumb, George F. Scheer (editor). *Yankee Doodle Boy: A Young Soldier's Adventures in the American Revolution Told by Himself.* Holiday House, 1995.

Stewart, Gail B. *The American Revolution: Life of a Soldier in Washington's Army* (American War Library). Lucent, 2002.

Tibbitts, Alison Davis. *John Paul Jones: Father of the American Navy* (Historical American Biographies). Enslow, 2002.

Places to Visit

Valley Forge National Historical Park
P. O. Box 953
Valley Forge, PA 19482-0953
Telephone: (610) 783-1077

Web Sites

Camp Followers in the American Revolution
users.erols.com/grippo/campfol.html
Essay about camp followers by living history enthusiast Laura Webb Thomas.

Excerpts from the Diaries of Joseph Plumb Martin
www.mrbooth.com/edu/constit/ diaries.html#2
Part of an educational unit about the U.S. Constitution, these pages reproduce part of the journal of Revolutionary soldier Joseph Plumb Martin. Also includes shorter excerpts from Continental army officer Ebenezer Denny and Valley Forge surgeon Albigence Waldo.

The Revolution's Black Soldiers
www.americanrevolution.org/blk.htm
Web page about African-American revolutionary soldiers from history web site.

Women Spies – Miss Jenny
www.si.umich.edu/spies/stories- women–1.html
Account of British spy Miss Jenny from "Spy Letters of American Revolution," an online exhibition from the University of Michigan's Clements Library.

Index